Sand Castles
Step-by-Step

Lucinda Wierenga
with
Walter McDonald

Photography by Del Hoppe
Illustrations by Alan Carrington

Meadowbrook Press
Distributed by Simon & Schuster
New York

Library of Congress Cataloging-in-Publication Data

Wierenga, Lucinda.
    Sand castles step-by-step / Lucinda Wierenga, Walter McDonald ;
  illustrations by Alan Carrington.
          p.   cm.
    1. Sand craft.   2. Sand castles.   3. Sand sculpture.   I. McDonald,
  Walter.   II. Title.
  TT865.W54   1989   89-13906   736'.9—dc20

ISBN: 0-88166-128-7

Production Editor: Sandy McCullough
Art Director: Kevin Bowen
Production Manager: David Garbe
Cover and interior design: Dan Norquist

Simon & Schuster Ordering #: 0-671-69611-4

Published by Meadowbrook Press, 18318 Minnetonka Boulevard, Deephaven, MN 55391.

BOOK TRADE DISTRIBUTION by Simon & Schuster, a division of Simon and Schuster, Inc., 1230 Avenue of the Americas, New York, NY 10020.

90 91 92 93 5 4 3 2 1

Printed in the United States of America.

Contents

Sons of the Beach Pledge

Thus far we have managed to keep the secret of our sand castling success to ourselves by revealing it only to other SOBs. We do not intend to stray from this policy, so before you read any further, we must ask you to take a minute to raise your right hand and repeat the SOB pledge: I promise to have fun, help others have fun, and unlitter. (Unlittering is the exact opposite of littering; specifically, "to properly dispose of more garbage than you generate.")

Preface

We're the Sons of the Beach, a "not-profitable disorganization" headquartered on South Padre Island, Texas. Our island is composed of some of the finest sand castle-building material in the country, and we build a *lot* of sand castles—one or two a week, all year round—for which we have won a modest amount of fame. In fact, we hold the record for the longest sand sculpture in the world, the 10,760 foot-long *Millerpede,* as noted in the 1989 and 1990 editions of the *Guinness Book of World Records.*

There are several other professional sand sculptors throughout the United States and each team of sculptors has its own distinctive style. Our castles are distinguished by lofty towers and soaring arches, intricately carved and connected by fortified walls and winding staircases. Every SOB castle is a signed original, marked with the "Hooktail Texas"—a depiction of the Lone Star State with an elongated tail that ends in an arrow pointing at South Padre Island.

Amazin' Walter and myself—known collectively as the SOB Sand Castle Wizards—developed our distinctive technique of building over several years. Neither of us has ever had any formal training in art or architecture. We did not start playing in the sand with the idea that we would make a living at it. We built sand castles mainly because it gave us an excuse to hang out at the beach. We thought it was pretty neat when we won a few bucks at a local sand castle contest, but when someone asked us to build in a certain place at a specific time, we were thrilled to discover that people would actually *pay* us to do something that we were already doing just for fun!

Since 1985 we have built castles for beach parties, advertising promotions, and TV broadcasts. We have built 100-ton sand-castle billboards and miniature castles constructed in boxes and sprayed with glue to be used as door prizes. We've built in shopping malls, on fairgrounds, in convention centers, and in hotel lobbies. In 1988 we built a total of 51 commissioned sand castles—nearly one a week. On our days off we walk over to our favorite local beach and build for fun. If the beach is crowded, we experiment on the pile of sand in our front yard. Since we live on a modified sandbar, there is never a shortage of building material.

One day not too long ago we looked up from a castle and noticed that we were having more fun than just about anyone else on the beach. More specifically, *they* were all standing around watching *us!*

Now, it's a well-known fact (at least around here) that a single SOB can have more fun than any ten non-SOBs in any given situation. In an attempt to balance this inequitable state of affairs, it occurred to us that swearing in new SOBs and teaching them how to sand castle might just be the way to help others have fun. So we wrote this book hoping that others will use it, expand upon it, and share *their* secrets with us.

We'd like to stress here that sand castling is most fun when experienced as a group activity. A little bit of organization and leadership can go a long way toward making this a family experience in which everyone—toddler to grandpa—may partipate. If you are a parent, don't assume that merely handing this book to your children and saying, "Here kids, go out and build a masterpiece," is going to keep them out of your hair for the rest of the afternoon. This book is intended to be used in a situation involving adult supervision and *participation.*

To take this idea one step further, you don't *have* to have a child around to justify a sand castling experience. If you're looking at this book, we can safely assume that you have enough of a kid left in you to enjoy sand castling on its own merits.

If you *are* a kid, it should be a relatively easy task to secure your parents' assistance. If they balk, simply remind them of the importance of time spent together in fun activities, and ask if they would prefer that you quietly vegetate in front of the TV set instead. Use a lot of terms like "quality time," "familial interaction," and "parental responsibility." Once they've tried it they'll probably love sand castling, so make sure you score your own set of tools early in the game.

If you carefully read and follow the suggestions printed here, you will soon be building sand castles that will impress your friends and neighbors. If you practice these skills several times in the period of one year, you will soon be building sand castles that will impress a total stranger. If you continue to practice these skills once a week for the period of two years, you will be building sand castles that will impress *us.* Keep it up for another year or so, and you can write the sequel to this book.

If we don't beat you to it.

Lucinda "Sandy Feet" Wierenga
"Amazin'" Walter McDonald

1. Getting Started

Introduction

S.A.N.D. Therapy

Sand castling is good therapy—and it's a lot cheaper than psychoanalysis. We've found at least four good reasons to get involved in sand castling as a hobby. They are collectively known as S.A.N.D.: Sociability, Activity, Nonsense, and Daylight.

Sociability. It's easy to feel lonely in the middle of a crowd, but it is nearly impossible to feel lonely when you're in the middle of a great sand castle. People are drawn like magnets to beach art, and they are convinced that you, the creator, must be a terribly fascinating person.

Activity. Less strenuous than volleyball but more so than shell-hunting, sand castling involves a good deal of bending over, lifting, and stretching.

Nonsense. "All that effort—just to see it stomped on or washed away by the tide!? What's the point?" "Mud pies are for kids." "Some people just refuse to grow up." These are all comments you can expect to hear while sand castling. As a rule American adults are malnourished when it comes to nonsense, and we maintain that sand castling is one of the most therapeutic forms of nonsense around. Granted, we have nothing upon which to base our theory other than our own sense of well-being, which is considerable.

Daylight. It is a well-known fact that we humans thrive on sunlight. Studies suggest that a daily dose of sunshine can do wonders for a person's outlook on life. Millions of sun-worshippers agree that the beach, any beach, is the best place to catch a few rays. And sand castling is one the best reasons we've discovered yet for hanging out on the beach.

It's Fun!

Of course, the *real* reason for sand castling can be stated much more succinctly—it's FUN! After all, going to the beach is one of America's favorite pastimes. Instead of just lying around in all that sand, why not play with it?

From our experience, lack of creativity is the most common excuse people give for not indulging in sand castling. But keep in mind that sand castling is *not* a test, it's just *playing in the sand*—not a very intimidating thought! You can build a primitive castle in a matter of minutes, but with some technical knowledge and a little practice, you'll find you have the potential to create a masterpiece. You don't need a license, a degree, or formal art training to build a better sand castle—you just need the tools and know-how to get you started. In addition to building techniques, the following pages are loaded with ideas that will make your sand castles satisfying to build and spectacular to behold.

What You Need

Sand

We have tried our method of building sand castles, with varying levels of success, on beaches all over the country. Some builders give sand the slump test, which measures the sand's ability to stand in structural form. We, however, prefer the juggle test. We scoop up three handfuls of super-wet sand and toss them around in the air. The longer we can juggle them, the better the sand is for sand castling.

The sand found on the beaches of the Texas Gulf Coast juggles very well. It contains sand mixed with silt from the Mississippi River and forms some very sticky stuff that can be stacked relatively easily into towers six feet tall.

East Coast sand is grainier and a bit more difficult to use. We were still able to stack towers and arches without much trouble, but to build more than three feet high, we had to pile up a very large base. We also found this to be true with the lake sand in Michigan.

As a general rule, the finer the sand, the better it stacks.

Water

Easy access to water is every bit as important as the quality of the sand, since water is what holds the sand together. You can build an impressive sand castle in a sandbox, as long as you have a garden hose within arm's reach.

Tools

One of the best things about our style of sand castling is that you can do it—with no advance preparation—almost anywhere there's a steady supply of sand and water.

When we first started building castles, we used our hands to dig the hole, build the structure, and smooth it. This method worked well enough, but eventually it dawned on us that some simple tools could help us build bigger and better sand castles with far less wear and tear on our hands.

We still maintain that anyone can build a very fine castle *au naturel,* and it's not a bad way to get started. But if you really want to build something that stands out on a crowded beach, we suggest you try some tools.

We always keep an eye open for carving tools that will do something different, but we've found most of our favorite tools just lying around in the garage or the kitchen.

Shovel. Since you will be digging a hole, using some type of shovel can save you both time and a manicure. A small garden spade works well if you're planning to build a small castle. An army surplus trenching shovel with a fold-down handle and adjustable blade is handy for carrying to the beach. A larger shovel will make the digging go faster still. But remember: the size of the shovel is directly proportional to the stress on your back. Don't overdo it; you're supposed to be having fun!

Buckets. Buckets always come in handy. We use one to carry our carving tools and another to hold extra water in case we build far away from the hole we dug, or we build an extraordinarily tall tower. We also like to keep a bucket of water sitting around to rinse the sand off our hands.

Trowels. Use a mason's trowel to take the bumps out of walls and big towers. The offset handle makes it ideal for smoothing large, vertical expanses, such as walls on which you want to carve messages.

Kitchen and Putty Knives. Knives come in a variety of shapes and sizes and experimenting with different ones can be lots of fun. Shaping the sand by hand creates very interesting effects, but to get hard edges you'll need knives. Use a long knife for squaring off towers and a small knife for detail work. Putty knives work well for scraping out doors and windows. If you have a small child with you, remember that putty knives also come in plastic.

Melon Baller or Ice-Cream Scoop. Use these handy tools to carve round windows and scalloped edges.

Optional Tools. You may also want to bring along a paintbrush for finely detailed carving and lettering; a toy rake or brush for sweeping up excess sand when the castle is finished; and a household spray bottle for spraying the castle with water, glue, or paint.

Picking a Spot

Our method of building sand castles starts with digging a hole until you reach wet sand. So pick a spot where your castle will look good and you can dig down to get all the wet sand you'll need. Choosing where to dig your hole can be tricky, especially if you are building on a shoreline that is subject to tides. If you dig too close to the waterline and the tide happens to be coming in, your sand castle could suffer an early and tragic demise. On the other hand, if you dig too far away from the waterline and the tide happens to be going out, you'll have to dig a *very* deep hole to reach water, wearing yourself out before you even get started. If you are extremely thorough, you will consult a tide chart, date footprints, and carefully plot the exact spot for your castle.

We use a slightly less scientific method ourselves. In general, we look for a higher patch of beach close to the waterline. These spots are the last to get swamped when the tide comes in, and they also give your castle a little extra height.

Different beaches have varying amounts of trash. Nothing detracts from a splendid castle like a mess of unsightly soft-drink cans strewn around it. Follow your pledge to "unlitter" and do yourself and your spectators a favor by unlittering the area before you even start. There's a chance that others will follow your example, or at least be more conscious of their own trash.

You may also want to think ahead to when you photograph your finished castle. Keep in mind the position of the sun and the background for your photograph as you choose your spot. For more hints, see our chapter called "Photography" at the end of the book.

Once you have picked your spot and staked your claim, you are ready to get down to the nitty-gritty—and we do mean GRITTY!

Our Dribble Method

There are many different ways to build sand castles, and every way has its advantages and constraints. Below is a brief review of the simplest and most widely used methods.

Plastic molds have recently come into vogue. Designed primarily for kids, molds allow you to quickly put up a structure that is immediately identifiable as a sand castle. Molded towers require no carving, but soon even small children discover their limitations: no altitude and no variety. A tower from a mold can only stand as tall as the mold, and every tower that comes from a mold looks pretty much like every other tower from that mold.

The most common technique used by serious sand castle builders is the pile method. Builders start by digging a moat around a pile of sand, which they wet down by lugging buckets of water from the ocean, lake, or pond. This method usually involves more work than most casual sunbathers care to do.

Nearly anyone who has spent any time on a beach has experimented with the dribble method. You just sit down right by the water, scoop up a handful of dripping-wet sand, and let it dribble off your fingertips. Dribbling is fun and easy, but it too has its limitations. You can't get a lot of height or mass by dribbling, and one good wave is all it takes to wipe out your castle.

We describe our technique as a modified dribble method. Instead of using wet sand at the waterline, we dig a hole in drier sand until we hit water. We then pull dripping-wet sand from the hole and stack it one handful at a time. This method requires less preparation and far less work than the pile method, but gives you more flexibility than mere dribbling. Stacking achieves great height and mass and your castle is positioned where it is less likely to get wiped out by waves.

Why doesn't everybody build sand castles this way? As far as we know, we invented this method. After a little practice we discovered that two of us could beat a six-member team quite handily in a sand castle contest. That is called brain over brawn.

Once you are familiar with the basic building and carving techniques described in the first part of this book, you might want to try some of the suggestions that follow them. Most beach communities hold sand castle contests—South Padre Island schedules at least three every year. Most of our suggestions are proven judge-pleasers, and they can help catapult you or your team into the winner's circle.

Preparing the Base

This is the point where our style of building sand castles differs from others; we have yet to find anyone else who starts with a hole rather than a pile. As far as we know, we invented the idea—mostly out of sheer laziness.

Digging a hole serves two purposes. First, the loose sand from the hole gives you a firm base upon which to build your first tower, protecting your castle from meltdown. Second, the hole gives you an immediate source of water. You see, it isn't the *sand* that holds a sand castle together, it's the *water*.

Water—lots of it—is absolutely essential to sand castling. If you dig a hole in the sand, you'll eventually hit water. Any sand you draw from that hole will come out premoistened, and that beats lugging buckets any day!

There is no reason why you can't build a castle right at ground level, but the more height your castle has, the more impressive it will be. Pile the sand from your hole in one spot to serve as the base for your tallest tower.

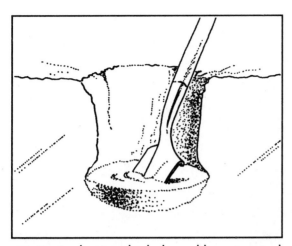

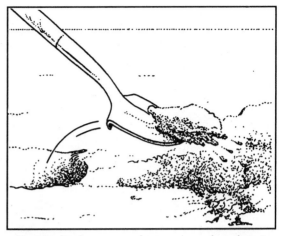

1 Begin digging the hole and keep in mind that you are aiming for *depth,* not *width.* Once you hit water the hole will grow wider all by itself as the water eats away at the edges.

2 Pile the loose sand in a mound, at least a foot away from your hole to compensate for the hole's tendency to spread. This pile will eventually serve as the base for your first tower.

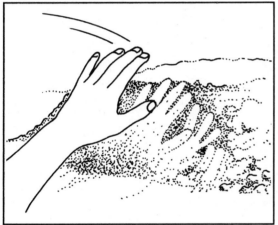

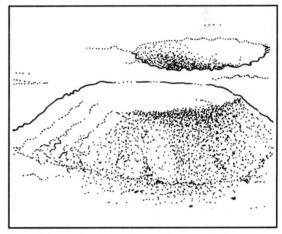

3 Pack the loose sand as tightly as you can by slapping the sides of the mound with the flat of your hand.

4 Flatten the top of your base, and you are ready to start building.

Since this sand came from the surface of the beach, it will be drier than the sand you use to do the actual building, and would be nearly impossible to carve. If you want to carve your tower all the way to ground level, you might want to use the shovel handle to jab some holes in the top of your base mound and pour buckets of water into the mound until it is saturated. This step, however, is not necessary for first attempts. If any casual beach strollers ask you if you are digging for buried treasure or your keys, the correct response is, "Watch the pile, not the hole."

Achieving Altitude

The primary aim of every sand castler, from established pros right down to the kids in the sandbox, is to build that castle as high as possible. The reason most people have a problem reaching the heights they want is because they do not use enough water. Achieving the correct ratio of sand to water is the secret to building a tall sand castle.

It is not difficult to work the water into the sand. When you are working from a hole dug down to the water, you'll find it fairly simple to maintain the right consistency, provided that you keep mixing the sand and water. A cement mixer would do the trick quite handily, but would be difficult to take to the beach. Actually, the best tools for this job are your feet.

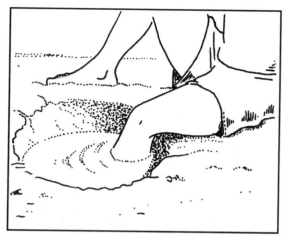

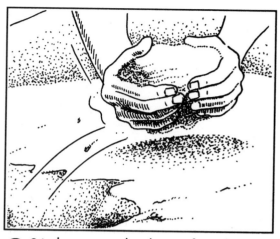

1 Position yourself so you are sitting on the edge of the hole, with one foot in the water.

2 Stir the wet sand with your foot, then quickly scoop out a large handful and pour it onto the base.

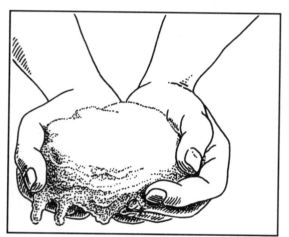

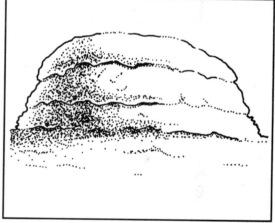

3 Scoop out sand that has the consistency of oatmeal. It should be practically dripping through your fingers and wet enough to settle into something like a flat pancake.

4 Pour one pancake on top of another. The water draining from the top bonds the two pancakes together, giving your structure a certain amount of stability.

If you crave immediate success in sand castling, put a rein on your ambition. Start small, testing the limitations of the sand as you go. Accept the fact that you are probably not going to achieve a six-foot tower the first time you try. If you can build a one-foot tower on your first attempt, you're doing very well.

Building a Tower

There are three basic building units in a sand castle: the tower, the wall, and the arch. Once you are successful with all three, you can combine them to create a variety of architectural structures.

The tower is the first basic unit of the sand castle. Everything else is a variation on that theme. Don't despair if your first few attempts look feeble; if you're able to build a solid, one-foot-tall tower in your session, you should feel proud of yourself and be ready to build one two feet tall the next time. Once you can build a good, solid tower, the fancy stuff will come a lot easier.

As you build keep in mind that the more water you have in the sand, the longer the tower will last. Remember also that a large base helps you build higher, carve more easily, and be more creative with your structure.

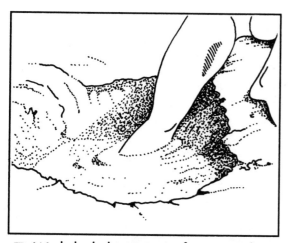

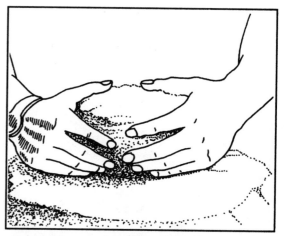

1 Work the hole. Use your foot to stir the wet sand at the bottom until you have a puddle about the same consistency as oatmeal.

2 Scoop up a large handful of wet sand from the puddle and pour it onto the base mound, holding it around the edges and jiggling it gently as it settles onto the base.

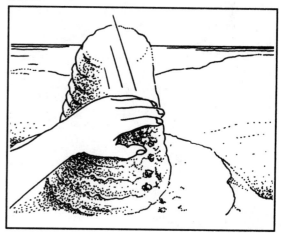

3 Keep stirring the wet sand with your foot and stacking handfuls of wet sand, gradually reducing their size so that the tower tapers at the top. The end result should look something like a stack of fat pancakes.

4 To get rid of the pancake look, gently scrape the length of the tower with the edge of your hand, smoothing it all the way down.

Having problems getting a tower to stand? Try starting from a bigger base, and don't be too ambitious until you start getting a feel for what the sand will and will not do. Be sure you taper off as you build—if you don't, the tower will be top-heavy. Check your sand. It should flatten out like a pancake. If it doesn't, it probably isn't wet enough. It should be dripping between your fingers as you lift it out of the hole. Don't push, pummel, or shake your tower, and when it starts looking precarious, stop building.

Building a Wall

Walls are used for many different purposes in building sand castles. At the simplest level, you can build walls around a castle to function as a fence. You can weave walls into and around towers and arches to join them into a unit, or build taller walls to serve as billboards upon which to carve messages, logos, or names.

Building a wall with sand is much like building a wall with bricks—the main difference is that you are forming your own bricks out of sand as you lay them. For ideas on finishing touches for walls, see the section on carving.

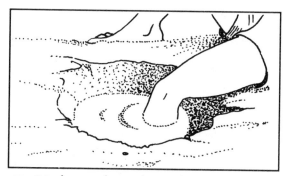

1 Stir the sand to achieve the proper consistency. Scoop out a handful and lay it in a clump.

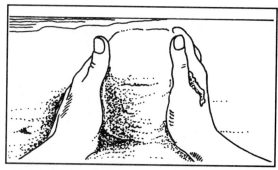

2 Mold the clump into a brick-like shape by holding your hands flat on both sides of it as the water drains.

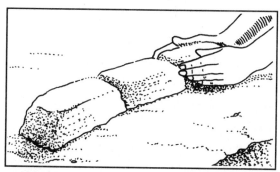

3 Repeat with more handfuls of sand, laying the "bricks" end to end along the line where you want your wall to go.

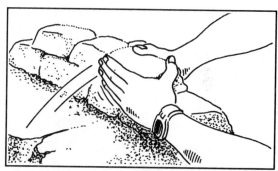

4 Lay another layer of bricks on top of the first, positioning them so they cover the joints in the bottom layer.

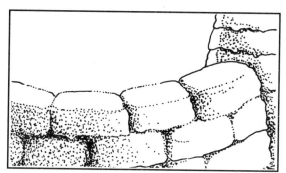

5 Continue layering until the wall reaches the desired height.

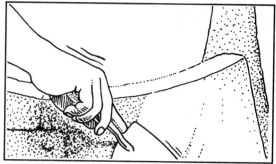

6 Smooth the wall with your hands, a table knife, or a trowel—or just leave it rugged-looking.

Building an Arch

By far the most remarkable element of the sand castle is the sand arch. Walter developed his arch technique over five years ago, and it continues to amaze people because the arches look like they must use some kind of support system such as wires or stakes.

Walter builds his arches the same way the Romans did, the same way any architect will tell you to build one—with a keystone. If you follow these instructions, you'll soon be building with the keystone method, too.

Here's one word of warning: do *not* attempt to build an arch before you can successfully build a tower.

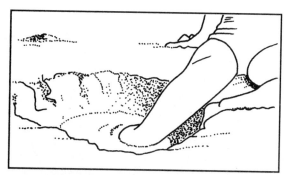

1 Stir the wet sand in the bottom of your hole until it reaches the proper consistency.

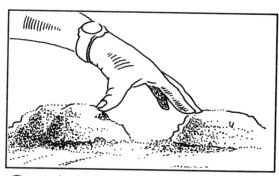

2 Lay the bottom pancakes of two towers, about three inches apart, and construct a stable base for each tower.

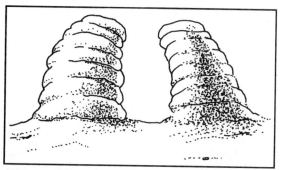

3 Continue building so the towers lean toward each other, until it looks as though they are about to topple over.

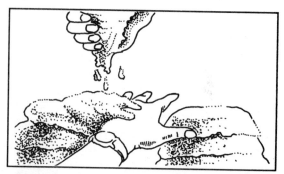

4 Bridge the gap between them with the back of your free hand. Pile wet sand over your hand.

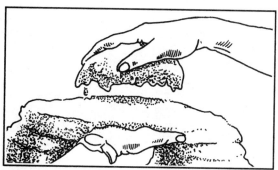

5 The last handful of sand is the keystone that holds the arch together. Gently place the keystone where the two towers meet.

6 Continue supporting the keystone with your hand for a few seconds as the sand settles, then withdraw your hand slowly.

If you suffer from fallen arches, reread the instructions and try again, using smaller towers. As you gain experience, your success rate will improve dramatically. Using the keystone method you will soon build arches two to three feet tall. Building a solid arch takes practice. It's a *simple* process, but not an *easy* one.

Combining Arches

Walter has been building sand arches for so long that he makes it look like child's play—but building a solid arch takes practice. As Walter says, "It's a *simple* process, not an *easy* one." Once you have had some success with arches, try experimenting with variations in their size, shape, and mass. The next step is to combine several arches for an impressive architectural effect. See the next page for more ideas.

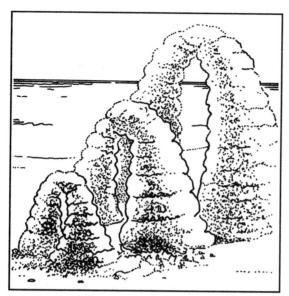

1 Increase the distance between the two towers to add height to your arch. This, however, will also make the gap more difficult to span.

2 Create a spidery-looking structure by building a circle of arches that fan out from one tower.

3 Form a bridge by building a series of arches base to base. Smooth the top of each arch with a knife or a trowel.

4 Create an arched walkway between towers by building a series of arches in a row.

Combining Structures

When you have mastered the techniques for building towers, walls, and arches, you can combine these basic units to create any number of unusual and whimsical structures.

On the facing page are some combinations we've come up with. Try them out, then use your imagination and create your own.

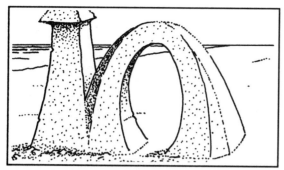

Arch and Towers. Build extra-large bases capable of supporting a tower and one trunk of the arch.

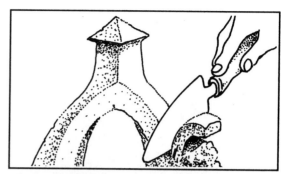

Arch with Topknot. Add a small tower to the top of a sturdy arch.

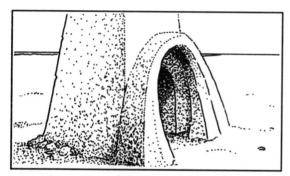

Tower with Arched Doorway. Build a small arch so that it leans against a tower's base.

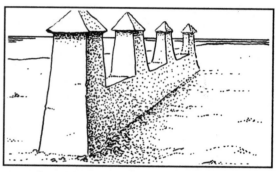

Fortified Watchtower. Build a thick wall to support a tower. Or, build a tower first, then build a wall in front of or adjacent to it.

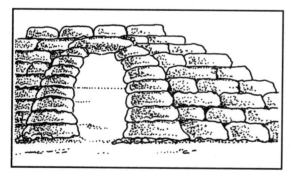

Arched Gateway. Build the arch first, then build the wall adjacent to and over it.

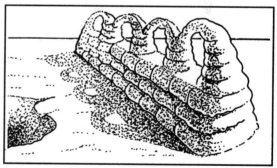

Coliseum. Build a series of small arches, base to base, on top of a sturdy wall.

Putting It All Together

If you can attain any height at all, each of these structures can be quite impressive in itself. But connected into a unified castle, these structures can be positively awesome. Your final castle can take on any shape you want it to, depending on its function.

You can build a series of towers and arches around your trench, perhaps connected by walls that weave in and out of the other structures. This gives the castle the appearance of a fortified city with lots of open gateways.

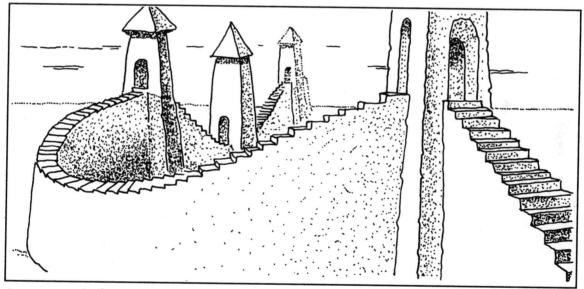

Staircases are also a great way to connect structures. Spectators are thrilled by staircases even though they are very easy to build. Simply connect two towers with a wall that slopes like a ramp, then cut out the stairs with a small knife (kids: use a plastic or putty knife). Page 34 has more information on carving staircases.

3. Sculpting and Carving

The Basics of Carving

Carving a sand castle is like icing a cake—both take patience and a steady hand, and both profoundly improve the aesthetic appeal of the finished product. Anyone who's tried icing a cake that hasn't been properly baked knows it's difficult. In the same way, a tower that hasn't been properly built is hard to carve. A solid, massive tower is much easier and much more fun to carve than a small, feeble one. The best plan is for either you or your partner to master building structures first.

As we said earlier, you *don't* need formal schooling in art to carve beautiful towers. Anyone can do a capable carving job. Clean, smooth lines take very little imagination, yet they transform a ho-hum tower into something truly magnificent. You might even find hidden reserves of talent and creativity emerging as you gain experience.

The first and most important rule when carving any structure built of sand and water is to start at the top. Should you ignore this rule and start somewhere else, you'll soon discover that gravity is your enemy; loose sand from your carving can quickly obliterate the fine detail of your work.

Second, don't hack or chip away at the structure. First-time carvers often make the mistake of timidly chipping away at the tower for hours until there is nothing left. Instead, slice with long, clean strokes.

Be careful not to undercut the base to a smaller diameter than the top, and keep in mind that sand, unlike clay, cannot be patched. Once it's sliced away, it's gone for good. This tendency makes it difficult to plan your carving in advance. The sand doesn't always cooperate, so you must adjust your ideal vision to the working conditions you encounter.

Sculpting by Hand

What if the need to sculpt a sand master-piece arises on a deserted beach—with no hardware store in sight? Can it be done? Certainly. Hands are very suitable tools.

Their use for carving is somewhat limited, but you can still create many interesting shapes using only your hands.

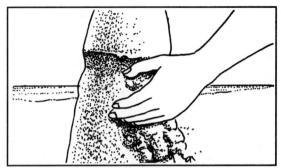

Smoothing. An unadorned tower should resemble an untidy stack of cow patties. Smooth off the rough stuff by gently running your hands down the sides, allowing the loose sand to fall to the tower's base. The resulting surfaces should be even and smooth.

Shaping. One way to enhance the shape of a tower is to remove sand from selected areas. Create a roof-like structure by scraping sand from around the edges of the top to form a conical shape. Then remove more sand from the bottom of the cone, smoothing all the way down to highlight the tower's tapering shape.

Decorating. Use individual fingers to create interesting patterns on the smooth walls. Run your index finger down one side of the tower to form an indentation extending from the base of the roof to the bottom of the tower. Repeat at regular intervals all around the tower.

Carving with Tools

You can create very interesting shapes with your bare hands, but to get the straight, hard edges and intricate detail that will really impress the neighbors, you'll need tools. Our favorite tools are listed in the "What You Need" section. The following instructions for carving with tools are merely suggestions for getting started. Once you get the hang of it, you'll undoubtedly come up with interesting variations of your own. Don't be afraid to try new and radical ideas!

The Square Tower

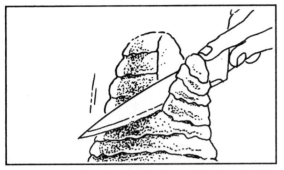

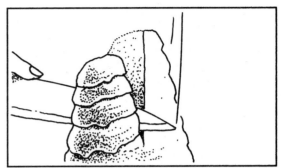

1 Start at the top with a large kitchen knife (kids: use a plastic knife or putty knife). Shave off excess sand to create a four-sided structure.

2 Practice the long, clean strokes we mentioned earlier.

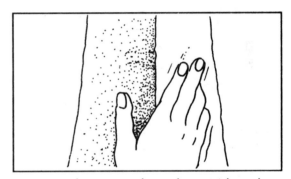

3 Slice off the top so that it is also square.

4 Smooth any rough patches gently with your fingertips.

The Pyramid Tip

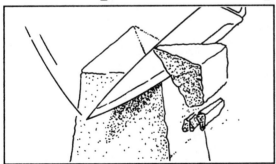

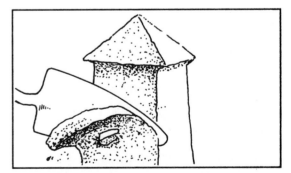

1 Start at the top of the tower and use a large knife (kids: use a putty knife) to slice four sides at an angle, keeping them fairly even. Do this until you have formed a pointed tip and are satisfied with the pyramid's shape.

2 Define the base of the pyramid by making horizontal slices on all four sides and cutting away layers below the base so the tower narrows before it reaches the pyramid. Don't be discouraged if you lose a corner. Making pyramid tips becomes easier with practice.

The Balcony

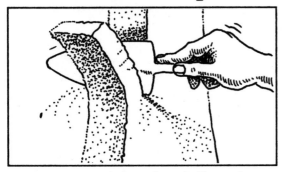 

1 Cut a vertical slice about halfway down the tower's length; then cut horizontally at the base of the first cut to form a giant step.

2 Make a second horizontal cut about an inch under the first one and scrape back the sand below to make it even with the wall above the balcony. This forms a ledge that juts out from the rest of the tower.

 Choose one side of a tower for a balcony. Since very few towers are symmetrical, look for a side that is bulkier than the others.

Doors

 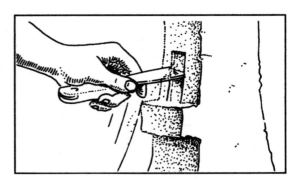

1 Insert the flat end of a putty knife into a wall a couple of inches above a balcony and scrape downward, removing a thin layer of sand.

2 Repeat the motion, this time scraping from bottom to top. Keep scraping in alternate directions until you achieve the desired depth.

A putty knife works well for details like doors and windows.

Windows

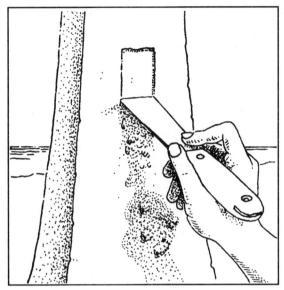

1 Carve rectangular windows by using the same techniques described for carving doors.

2 Make round windows with a putty knife. Rotate the handle gently until you have a smooth, even, circular indentation.

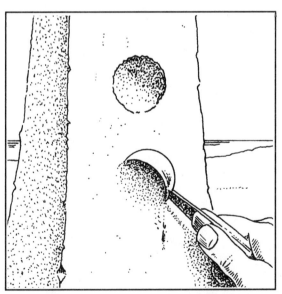

3 Use a melon baller or ice cream scoop to scoop out round windows.

4 Combine circles and rectangles to form arched doorways and windows.

The Staircase

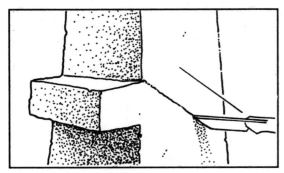

1 Start on one side of your balcony. Insert the tip of your knife (kids: use a table knife) horizontally into the tower and make a cut in the sand at a downward angle, following the shape of the tower.

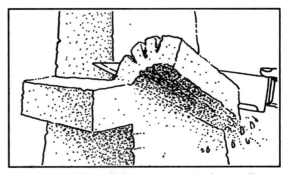

2 Go back and slice or scrape the wall above the ramp so that it juts out, similar to the balcony, only sloped.

3 Use a small knife or table knife to make a vertical slice, about an inch deep, at the top of the ramp.

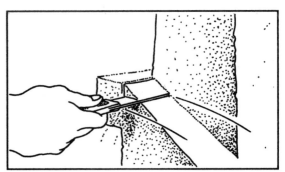

4 Make a horizontal slice at the base of the vertical slice, and you have a step!

5 Alternate vertical and horizontal slices for the length of the ramp.

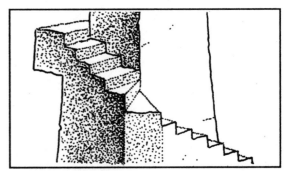

6 Either end the staircase with another balcony, or let it wind all the way down the tower in a spiral.

Tower Variations

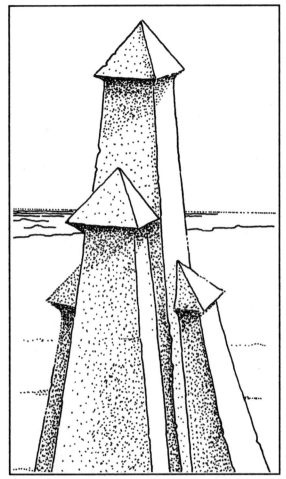

The Multi-Pyramid Tower

The Layered Tower

The Multi-Balconied Tower

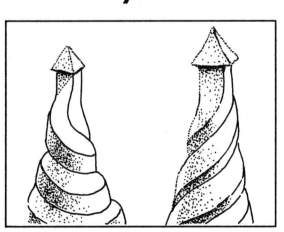

The Spiral Tower

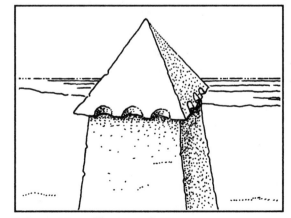

The Scalloped Tower

Carving an Arch

Generally speaking, anything that can be carved on a tower can also be carved on an arch. The arch, however, has a naturally graceful shape, and the astute carver will take advantage of this grace by emphasizing it. One very effective method for carving an arch is called "layering." Layers create shadows, and shadows give castle photographs more depth. Follow the steps on the next page to create a layered arch.

1 Use a large knife to slice and smooth all surfaces. (Kids: use a putty knife.)

2 Use a small, pointed knife or a putty knife to draw a line one inch from and following the outside curve of the arch.

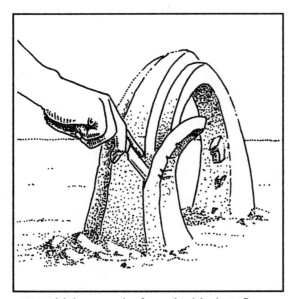

3 Hold the putty knife so the blade is flat to the arch's surface and slice away a layer of sand within the line. The deeper you slice, the more noticeable the layering effect will be.

4 If you like the look of one layer, try multiple layers or stripes.

Arch Variations

As creator of your castle, you are not bound by the narrow limits of conventional architectural design. There is no rule that says your layers have to be straight or that you have to follow any particular rules when building your castle.

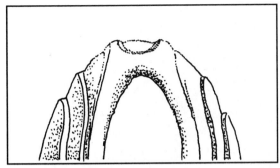

Swirlies. Cut a layer that swirls over and around your arch in fluid, three dimensional curves. Continue cutting layers that follow the original curves. This technique requires little thought but produces a very attractive effect.

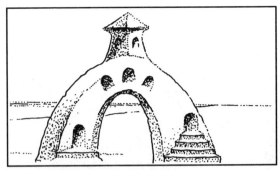

The Habitable Arch. Doors, windows, balconies, and staircases all help create an arch that any sand crab would be proud to call home. Topknotted arches work particularly well because you can carve a pyramid roof on the top.

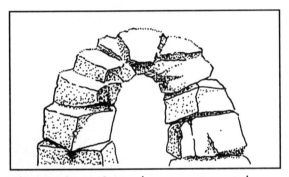

The Rock Arch. It takes some time to do a whole arch this way, but it's a very interesting effect. Square up the arch, then slice out crevices with a small, pointed knife or a putty knife so that your arch looks as though it was constructed from giant rocks or blocks.

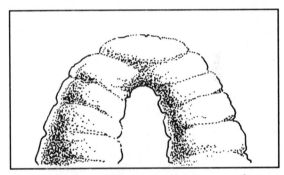

The Segmented Arch. This one can be done using only your hands. Smooth the arch's surfaces just enough to remove the roughness. Emphasize the points where individual handfuls meet by rubbing them with your fingertips.

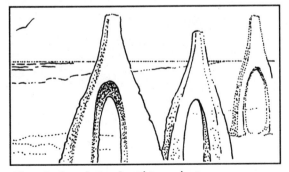

The Spired Arch. This technique creates a very graceful arch. Begin carving at the center of the span and slice each side to accentuate the natural slope of the sides. Leave a tall point in the center top of the arch.

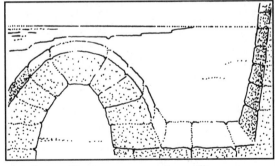

Brickwork. You can give a wall, tower, or arch a brick finish. Using a small, pointed knife, draw evenly spaced horizontal lines. Break up the horizontal stripes with short, vertical lines that simulate the look of bricks.

Bas-Relief Carving

When you carve in relief, you are carving only the surface or top layers. This is the safest kind of carving because it doesn't tamper with the arch or tower's structure. When carving in relief, you have more than one chance to do it right. If your first attempt is unsuccessful, you can just slice it off and try again—provided your surface is fairly thick.

1 Start with a relatively flat surface, such as one side of a squared-off tower or wall, and use a table knife or trowel to smooth the surface.

2 Etch the line or lines you wish to define with a small paring or putty knife. Try a star, a heart, or a diamond—something simple.

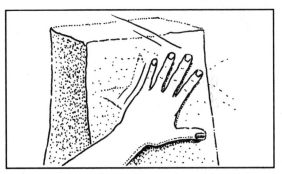

3 Erase your first attempt if you don't like it by smoothing it with your hand. Try again until you are satisfied with your design.

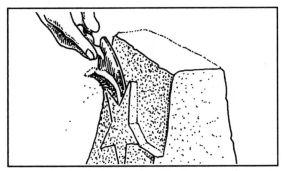

4 Hold the knife so the blade is flat against the surface and slice away the top layer of sand around the design.

5 Repeat until you reach the desired depth. As with layering, the deeper the cut, the better the contrast.

Lettering

Turn your ordinary sand castle into a message castle by carving words in bas-relief on a wall or tower. This is the nicest way we've found to personalize a gift: carve someone's name or a special date on a castle and take a picture of it to hang on the wall later. We have built message castles for many special people, events, and organizations—and we have an album full of photographs to help us remember them all.

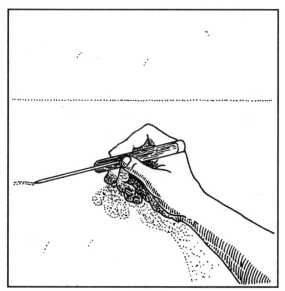

1 Etch a couple of parallel horizontal lines where you want the tops and bottoms of your letters to go. This step stops your message from traveling uphill or downhill and keeps your letters a uniform size.

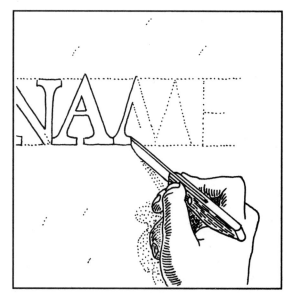

2 Etch in the letters lightly. Work with them until you feel satisfied with their shapes and spacing. The fatter the letters, the less likely they are to crumble.

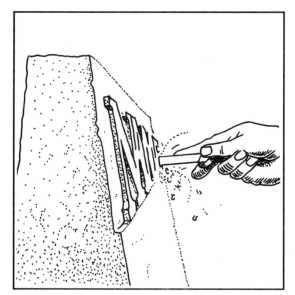

3 Shave away at the edges around the letters until they stand out in sharp relief from the flat surface.

4 Use a small, soft paint brush to dislodge loose sand between letters and obliterate any marks left by the carving process.

Faces

It is surprisingly simple to carve a recognizable face, and most beaches have plenty of live models from which to draw inspiration. A short, stubby tower works well for starters, but you can carve a face on most structures. Smaller heads require the use of smaller carving tools.

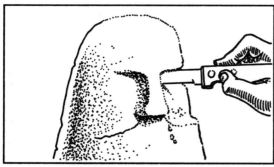

1 Start with the nose, since it protrudes farther than any other feature—on most faces, anyway. Define a roughly triangular shape by slicing away the sand around it.

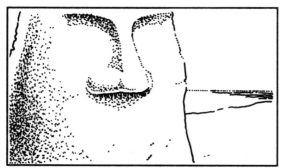

2 Give it a nose-like profile by shaving sand off the edges along either side of the nose's bridge. Define the nostrils.

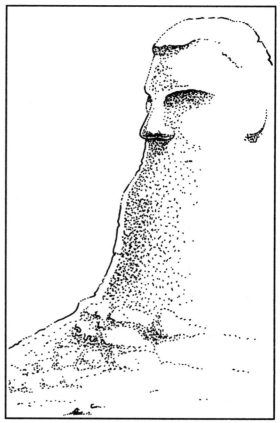

3 Smooth the expanse of the forehead, and hollow out indentations for eyes.

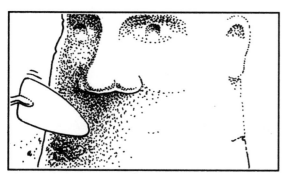

4 Define the cheekbones by hollowing out the cheeks underneath them.

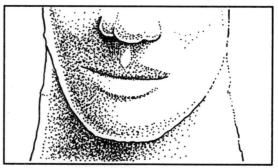

5 Carve the mouth, remembering that the lips and chin protrude slightly from the face's surface.

The trick to carving is knowing when to quit, and the only way to determine the limits of how much you can cut away is through experience. Even then, every once in a while a true masterpiece will dissolve into a nondescript pile of sand. When that happens, look upon the whole incident as a valuable learning experience and move on to the next tower.

4. Advanced Sand Castling

Sand Spheres

If you really want to cause a sensation, add sand spheres to your castle. We borrowed this nifty trick from some Japanese tourists on our home beach. The sand needs to be very sticky for it to work, but the method is easy if you have the right stuff. The resulting sand ball should be quite solid; we've seen them roll off four-foot towers and survive intact.

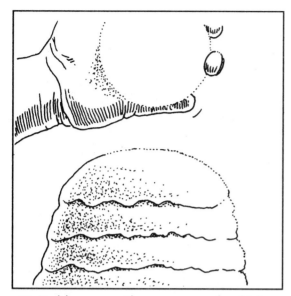

1 Build a tower. The tower must be thicker than the ball's diameter, or it might collapse.

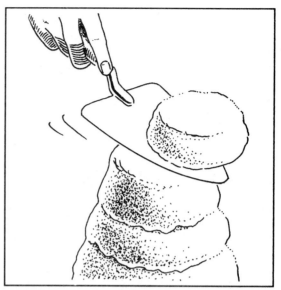

2 Slice the top off the tower or smooth it with your hands, creating a flat place on which to place the sphere.

3 Use your index finger to rub a small indentation in the flat top of the tower. This will ensure that the ball does not roll off.

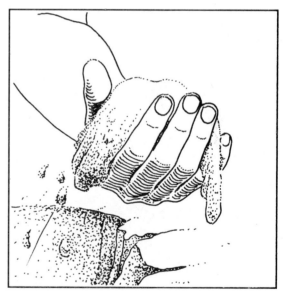

4 Stir the sand, then scoop up a handful of super-wet sand from the bottom of the hole. This is the core of the sphere.

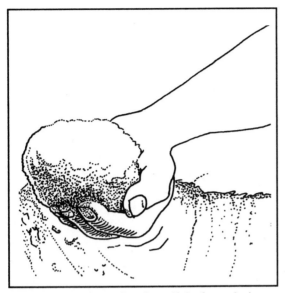

5 Scoop up another handful of sand, this time from the side of your hole where the sand is not so moist.

6 Combine the two handfuls, working the sand and packing it. You should have a solid—though soggy—sphere.

7 Find a patch of dry sand—the driest you can find—and roll the sphere in it, packing and polishing continually.

8 Place the sphere gently on the tower.

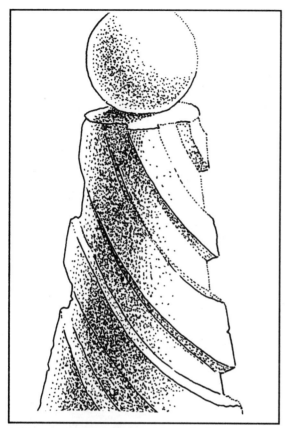

9 Carve the tower if you wish, but remember how heavy that ball is. If you undercut too much, the tower will become top-heavy and collapse.

10 Carve the ball itself if it is packed firmly enough. Try a spiky, three-dimensional star, a rounded heart, a smiling face, or anything else you can think of.

Tunnels

Tunneling through walls is easy. If your towers have fairly massive, solidly packed bases, you can also try tunneling through them. We have had good luck tunneling through walls, towers, and even the legs of some arches.

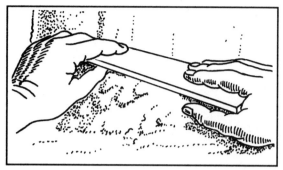

1 Smooth the surface of the wall with a trowel, a large knife, or your hands.

2 Use a small, pointed knife or putty knife to etch the opening of your tunnel.

3 Scoop out the sand with a knife. Long, slender knives work best, but kids should use plastic or table knives.

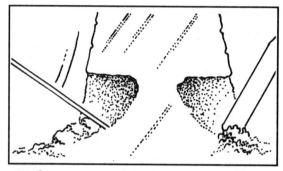

4 If you can reach both entrances to the tunnel, alternate your scoops between both ends, so you meet yourself in the middle.

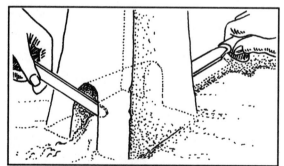

Base-of-Tower Tunnels. Tunneling through a tower works best if the base has plenty of water in it. Since the tunnel needs to be as long as the base is wide, you'll need a knife at least half that long. Use the technique described above, and dig from both sides.

Bisecting Tunnels. Once you have successfully tunneled through the base, add a second tunnel at right angles to the first. We have dug as many as three tunnels in a single, very large base.

 If you want to build a very large tunnel, try just building an arch into the wall.

Doors & Windows

If some part of your castle is too inaccessible or too small to accommodate an arch, try making an arched doorway or window instead. Be sure to start with a tower that has a large, smooth, squared-off base. You will be slicing the tower to make a wall.

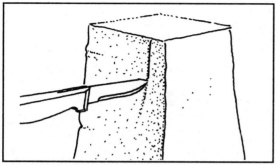

1 Etch a line down one side of the tower, set in at least an inch from the edge.

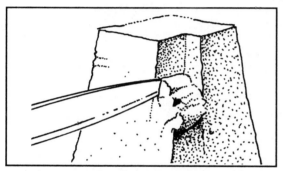

2 Use a small knife or putty knife to shave away sand along the edge of the line so that you have an indentation at least a couple of inches deep. This is one side of your wall.

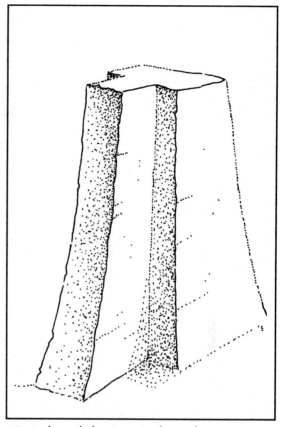

3 Etch and shave a similar indentation on the other side of the wall. Now you should have a two-sided wall, an inch or more thick, extending out from the rest of the tower.

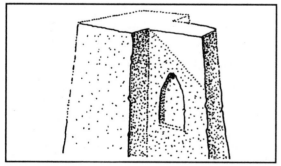

4 Scoop out an arch-shaped window in the wall with a small, slender knife. (Kids: use a table knife).

5 Combine a balcony with the wall and you can tunnel a doorway with the same technique.

Dyes & Decorations

Adding dyes or artificial decoration to a sand sculpture is definitely not for purists. Most competitions do not allow their use. However, here are some techniques you might want to try when you're feeling daring.

Dyes. Many serious builders have recently discovered just how eye-catching a colored sand sculpture can be. Sometimes such sculptures are garish, but tastefully applied colors can create interesting effects.

The easiest way to color a sand castle is to spray it with paint. Check the label on the spray paint to make sure it is nontoxic and biodegradable. Parents should handle any sprays or dyes for their children.

Other Decorations. We've seen sand castlers use a variety of objects to adorn their castles: paper flags; ceramic figurines; painted miniatures from role-playing games; plastic toys; and stuffed animals.

Our favorite decorations are those found on the beach naturally: shells, driftwood, and seaweed. And you don't have to lug them in or pick them up when you've finished.

Using Forms

We mentioned earlier the small plastic sand-packing forms for children. At the other end of the spectrum are the huge wooden contraptions constructed by professionals working for the big prizes. Somewhere in between there is a happy medium for the enthusiastic amateur.

Using forms has some obvious advantages. You can achieve greater heights with forms. You'll also find fewer air pockets because the sand is packed more firmly, making the structure easier to carve. On the other hand, using forms means lugging more hardware to the beach. In the interest of simplification, we rarely use forms—most jobs don't require them.

One way to limit the size of forms is to use a slip form, a shorter form you use repeatedly on the same structure. Similar to the technique used to set concrete, using slip forms requires two people—one to build and one to hold the form in place. The builder stacks wet sand inside the form while the partner holds the form and packs the sand on the sides of the tower. As the builder moves higher, the partner pulls the form up and packs the new layers of sand.

This method can work even without a form—just use the partners arms instead.

Cylindrical Forms

Most contest rules allow the use of forms, as long as you carve the resulting structure. If you want to try working with forms, you'll need a sturdy cylinder—a plastic trash can with the bottom cut out, a wide piece of PVC pipe, or reinforced cardboard tubing all work nicely. We've found that waterproof forms (with no seams for water to leak out of) work best. If you are working with a grainier sand, you may discover that even forms with seams will work well. For best results, you'll also need some sort of tamping device, such as a square piece of plywood with a perpendicular handle attached to the center of the square.

1 Shovel a layer of sand into the cylinder, then soak it with water until it is saturated.

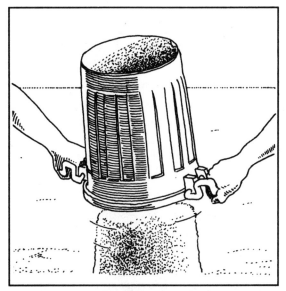

2 Alternate adding sand and water, packing the sand often with the tamping device, until you have filled the cylinder or reached the desired height.

3 Remove the cylinder by pulling it over the top. Do this *carefully*.

4 If you can't pull it off, cut open the side of the cylinder and unwrap the tower.

The resulting structure should be very sturdy and ready for carving. The drawback is that you may end up destroying a perfectly good trash can, and trash cans are not biodegradable. Depending on the condition of the sand, you may be able to tape the cylinder together and use it again.

Building from a Bucket

Sometimes digging out a hole to reach wet sand just isn't possible. Some contests, for example, plot out areas for the competitors that are too high for digging down to water. And the hole method doesn't work well if you're building in a sandbox or trying to build a castle higher than you can reach with your leg in a hole. As an alternative, you can build from a bucket.

If you must build out of a bucket, we recommend the large pickle buckets most restaurants dispose of every day. If you don't have a nearby water source, such as a hose, you'll need at least two buckets: one for mixing wet sand and another for toting water.

Shovel sand into the bucket, then fill the bucket with water. Keep working the sand with your hands to get the right consistency, and build as you would out of a hole. But watch your knuckles—you can scrape them pretty badly on the sides of the bucket and never realize the full extent of the damage until the next day.

5. Finishing Touches

Disguising the Hole

Not everyone is thrilled to have a gaping hole smack-dab in the middle of their masterpiece. If the hole is fairly shallow, you can often fill it in by simply sweeping into it loose sand from around the edges.

Deeper holes require more imaginative solutions. The easiest way to make a hole more attractive is to slice around the hole's rim with a large knife or trowel, and then smooth the ragged edges.

With enough time and diligence, you can finish off the hole by carving down into its sides. You can make towers or arches near the edges of the hole look much taller by extending their lines all the way down into the hole.

Another way to make the hole look more like part of the castle is to build an island in the middle of it. The easiest way to do this is to plan your strategy from the beginning and dig a ring instead of a hole. You can also build an island with wet sand from a bucket. Don't try building it with sand from the same hole or your island will get eaten away by the moving water faster than you can build it.

Preservation

Part of the sand castle's charm is its short life as an art object. You might manage to avoid the stompers, the frisbees, and the inquisitive people who just can't keep their hands to themselves ("Will it fall if I touch it like this? OOPS! Sorry..."), but don't forget the tide lying in wait, smacking its lips. It's rare for a castle to last overnight. You can't expect longevity from a mere pile of sand and water.

There are, however, several ways to extend a castle's short life span, should that be necessary. You can apply an additive to the castle in two ways: mix it in with the sand and water before you build; or spray it onto the finished castle.

If you only want your castle to survive a day or two, you might only need extra water. Any household-type sprayer will work. Just fill it up and soak the castle every hour. Small sprayers are hard on your hand, however, so if you plan a lot of spraying, consider investing in a larger pump model.

To make a castle survive as long as a week, you can use one part white glue added to three parts water. The glue, however, has a tendency to clog the sprayer nozzle, so wait and spray the whole thing at once, after you have finished building and carving—or else bring several sprayers along.

If you want to preserve a castle for an extended period of time, try mixing a concrete bonder with the sand. The stuff is too expensive to be practical on anything very large, but we've used it successfully on miniature demonstration castles, which we build from buckets into boxes measuring up to about a yard square. White glue can also be used, although it changes the texture of the sand, causing it to roll up in little balls instead of just falling to the bottom while you are carving, but the castles can last several months.

Other professional builders have had success using hairspray, clear acrylic, or epoxy to preserve their castles. The best plan is to experiment with different adhesives and see what works best with your sand. If you are working on a beach, *please* check the label to make sure that any additive you use is nontoxic and biodegradable.

Cleaning Up

As you carve, sand falls into piles around the base of the structure. An easy way to improve the castle's overall appearance is to clean up around it. Brush the loose sand back into the

hole or away from the castle. A child's toy rake is a great tool for this purpose. Sweeping back the loose sand gives your structure more thrust and its lines more definition.

6. Photography

Take a Picture

The easiest way by far to preserve a sand castle for posterity is to take a picture of it. Of course, no mere photograph is going to do justice to a real masterpiece. But the following photography tips will help you document your work on film, even with the cheapest camera on the market.

Before you go to the beach, take a few precautions to help protect your camera and your film. Sand can quickly destroy the internal mechanisms of your camera and hot sun will damage your film. Store your camera and film in a waterproof bag and a small cooler for protection between shots.

Shoot from a Low Angle

Photographing your sand castle from a low angle can make it look more impressive than it really is—if you don't mind wallowing in the sand a little. Get as low to the ground as your joints permit and shoot *up* at the castle. In addition to giving the structure greater thrust, this angle will serve to separate the castle from the surrounding sand, allowing it to stand out in sharper definition against the horizon. This technique will make you look like a real pro at both sand castling *and* photography.

Be Aware of the Background

The general rule for backgrounds is that less is better. The neutral scenery of the shoreline is preferable to a clutter of condos. The best plan, of course, is to shoot from a variety of angles. Just don't get so lost in shooting the subject that you forget about the background. And watch out for beach strollers who might wind up in your family album.

Fill Your Frame

These three words have become a kind of mantra, a litany we shout in chorus every time someone wants to take a picture of one of our castles. Family snapshots all too often feature an expanse of sky, miles of beach, and a tiny stick figure or two. ("Yup—that's Martha there...I think.") When you aim your camera, make sure you get as close as possible to the subject of your picture without cutting anything off. Also be aware of the shortest distance your camera can focus.

Include People, Too

Pretty pictures of pretty sand castles are very nice, but make sure you photograph the builders, too. If you ever want to prove to your brother-in-law that you were indeed the one who created such a beautiful castle, you'll need photos shot during its construction. Get plenty of shots of your family and friends as they build, and let them take some of you. Keep in mind that your castle will look taller if you ask your subjects to stoop or kneel around it.

The Sunlight Factor

Before you start your castle, you might want to consider where the sun is going to be when you finish, particularly if you have advanced to a castle with a message written on it. If you don't, you might find your detail washed out in sunlight or obscured in full shadow. Photograph castles with lettering late in the day, to take full advantage of the contrasts provided by late afternoon shadows. Lighting from the side provides the sharpest contrasts.

Taking pictures—lots of them!—is the only way to preserve a castle for eternity. If you get the chance, send one to us. Who knows? It might end up in the sequel to this book!

This photo shows the common mistakes people make when photographing sand castles. 1. The angle is too high. 2. The image does not fill the frame. 3. The sun is behind the castle, leaving the image in shadow. 4. The background is cluttered and detracts from the main image.

Conclusion

Over the past five years we have watched the popularity of sand castling as a hobby steadily increase. More families are discovering that building sand castles is a fun, active way to spend time together on the beach. And beachside communities are discovering that sand castle contests are a great way to draw vacationers during slow periods.

We have visions of someday setting a new world's record by building a castle, without the benefit of road graders or bulldozers, that is miles long. It would be great fun, and you're invited!

If you would like to get a sand castle event going in your favorite beach community, we would like to help. Contact the Sons of the Beach, P.O. Box 2694, South Padre Island, Texas 78597 for more information.

Strange But True Facts About Sex
by David Smith and Mike Gordon

Here's a book about sex that even Doctor Ruth could learn from. It contains strange but true and often hilarious facts from history, anthropology, medicine, and Hollywood gossip. Outrageous fun for trivia buffs and anyone fascinated by sex.
Order #4240

Dads Say the Dumbest Things
by Bruce Lansky and Ken Jones

Here's a hilarious book that has every funny (and stupid) expression fathers use to eduate and discipline their children...and drive them up the wall. It also includes 19 photos of TV's favorite fathers, plus humorous quotes from their TV shows.
Order #4220

Lucinda "Sandy Feet" Wierenga and "Amazin'" Walter McDonald can create a colossal customized sand castle to promote your special event.

Call toll-free, **800-338-2232,** or write for information about fees and scheduling:

Promotion Manager
Meadowbrook Press
18318 Minnetonka Blvd.
Deephaven, MN 55391

How to Survive High School...with Minimal Brain Damage
by Doug Lansky & Aaron Dorfman

This is the hilarious guide for high school students that Ferris Bueller would have written, if he wasn't so busy making a movie. It contains hundreds of pranks, hoaxes and dirty tricks. It's "the greatest invention for high school kids since Cliffs Notes."
—Dave Barry.
Order #4050

Weird Wonders & Bizarre Blunders
by Brad Schreiber

Here's a book for people who enjoy Guinness' most amazing records and Ripley's most unbelievable facts, but wish they went one step further into the zany zone. It's the weirdest collection of world records, and the funniest.
Order #4120

How to Survive Your 40th Birthday
by Bill Dodds

Bill Dodds shows those reaching middle-age that there's more to life after 40: old age and death. The book offers outrageous advice to those facing the bleak future.
Order #4260

The Unofficial College Dictionary
by Steve Zweig and Larry Cohen

Here's a college prep course every college-bound high school senior should take — a humorous guide to college life in dictionary form. There are 400 terms that every college student needs to know.
Order #4170

Order Form

Qty	Title	Author	Order No.	Unit Cost	Total
	Baby Name Personality Survey	Lansky/Sinrod	1270	$6.95	
	Best Baby Name Book	Lansky, B.	1029	$4.95	
	Best European Travel Tips	Whitman, J.	5070	$7.95	
	Dads Say the Dumbest Things	Lansky/Jones	4220	$5.95	
	Dictionary According to Mommy	Armor, J.	4110	$4.95	
	Discipline Without Shouting or Spanking	Wyckoff/Unell	1079	$5.95	
	Free Stuff for Kids, 14th Edition	FS Editors	2190	$4.95	
	How to Be a Catholic Mother	Dodds, B.	4230	$4.95	
	How to Survive High School	Lansky/Dorfman	4050	$5.95	
	How to Survive Your 40th Birthday	Dodds, B.	4260	$4.95	
	Italian Without Words	Cangelosi/Carpini	5100	$4.95	
	Parents' Guide to Dirty Tricks	Dodds, B.	4190	$4.95	
	Playing Fast & Loose with Time & Space	Mueller, P.	4100	$4.95	
	Pregnancy, Childbirth, and the Newborn	Simkin/Whalley/Keppler	1169	$10.95	
	Practical Parenting Tips	Lansky, V.	1179	$6.95	
	Shopping for a Better Environment	Tasaday	6150	$8.95	
	Sizzling Southwestern Cookery	Schroeder	6100	$6.95	
	Strange But True Facts About Sex	Smith/Gordon	4240	$6.95	
	The Unofficial College Dictionary	Zweig/Cohen	4170	$4.95	

Subtotal	
Shipping and Handling (see below)	
MN residents add 6% sales tax	
Total	

Meadowbrook Press

YES, please send me the books indicated above. Add $1.25 shipping and handling for the first book and $.50 for each additional book. Add $1.75 for each Read & Play Learning Set. Add $2.00 to total for books shipped to Canada. Overseas postage will be billed. Allow up to 4 weeks for delivery. Send check or money order payable to Meadowbrook Press. No cash or C.O.D.'s please. Quantity discounts available upon request. **Prices are subject to change without notice.**

Send book(s) to:
Name_____

Address_____

City_____ State_____ Zip_____

☐ Check enclosed for $_____, payable to Meadowbrook Press

☐ Charge to my credit card (for purchases of $10.00 or more only)

☐ Phone Orders call: (800) 338-2232 (for purchases of $10.00 or more only)

Account #_____ ☐ Visa ☐ MasterCard

Signature_____ Exp. date_____

Meadowbrook Press, 18318 Minnetonka Boulevard, Deephaven, MN 55391 (800) 338-2232